AFTER 86 SMITH STREET

AFTER
86
SMITH STREET

Joan Park

ISIS
LARGE PRINT
Oxford

First published in Great Britain 2004
by Isis Publishing Ltd.

Published in Large Print 2004 by ISIS Publishing Ltd,
7 Centremead, Osney Mead, Oxford OX2 0ES
by arrangement with the author

British Library Cataloguing in Publication Data
Park, Joan
    After 86 Smith Street. – Large print ed.
    (Isis reminiscence series)
    1. Park, Joan
    2. Large type books
    3. Liverpool (England) – Social life and customs
    – 20th century
    4. Liverpool (England) – Biography
    I. Title
    942.7'53082'092

ISBN 0–7531–9898–3 (hb)
ISBN 0–7531–9899–1 (pb)

Printed and bound by Antony Rowe, Chippenham

This book is written for my grandchildren,
Katherine, Rachel, Michael, Scott and Ross

Acknowledgements

I am indebted to the staff at Isis for their faith in an unknown writer of my vintage. I extend my gratitude to Jennifer Laurie, Kyle MacRae and Irene Marcuson for their criticism and encouragement at various stages of the writing. Above all I wish to thank my daughter and my son for their unstinted assistance in providing me with the word-processing tools and enough of their expertise to enable my scribble to become presentable. Finally I thank my sister, Thelma, who filled in so many gaps in my memory.

95 SOUTHDEAN ROAD

June 1934

I am nine years old, going on ten, and I am sitting on the low windowsill of my very own bedroom which I have all to myself for the very first time in my life.

It is one of the three bedrooms in our new house at 95 Southdean Road, part of a corporation housing scheme on the outskirts of Liverpool. The pavements are unfinished and all the road and building equipment is still at work a short distance away. We are the first people to live in this house and most of our neighbours have moved in before us.

Of course Granddad is still living at 86 Smith Street where we lived before we moved, because that is where his boot-repairing shop is and he still uses the ground floor and upstairs bedroom of the old Victorian house above and behind the shop.

Granddad spotted this housing scheme being built last May as, on one of his Wednesday half-days when the shop was closed, we rode to the terminus of the number 10 tramcar and walked the country lanes, gathering May blossom from the hedges. I won't forget that day in a hurry because it was the day Auntie Muriel took ill and was taken away to Rainhill Mental Hospital. Auntie Muriel is the younger of my father's two elder sisters. Auntie Gertie, the other sister, takes turns month about with us to have Auntie Muriel staying with her. Many times Mother has said that because Auntie Muriel suffers from her nerves she has from time to time to stay in Rainhill or Lancaster hospital for a rest. The big difference last May was that not only was my father away as usual, working as a bedroom steward on the Blue Funnel passenger ships, but Mother had gone away for a few days to help Auntie Gertie recover from a nervous breakdown. According to my mother, "Being married to Jack Hewitt has driven her to it and getting away from him to a village in Derbyshire could help."

Granddad sometimes worked in the shop as late as nine o'clock at night but he found the time to put a stew in the coal fire oven to cook slowly until the fire burned out. My sister, Thelma, and I set the table and washed up dishes and went the messages and my mother's best friend, Nurse MacKinlay, looked in sometime each day to see we were all right. When Nurse MacKinlay called, Auntie Muriel was usually washing herself in the bathroom or changing her dress or sitting doing her crochet which were the three things that occupied her for most of the day. Thelma and I had a bit of a giggle when Auntie joined us to go out for the afternoon, having powdered her face with what we recognised as Colgate's tooth powder, but one reproving glance from Granddad prevented us from sharing our observations with him.

When we returned home that evening and carried the May blossom indoors, even Granddad became fully aware that Auntie Muriel was upset. Despite his efforts to calm her, she raged and swore and directed blows to drive him away from her. It was all tremendously exciting, even after Thelma had been sent to fetch Nurse MacKinlay. She immediately banished us upstairs where we could still hear the shouting and the furniture getting knocked over and Auntie Muriel demanding that she see the girls. This seemed to go on for ages before strong men arrived in a van which took her away. When, on receiving Granddad's telegram, Mother returned home next day, Granddad urged her to put her name down for one of the new houses.

He comes up to see us whenever the shop is closed so he is with us on Wednesday afternoons, Sundays and Bank Holidays, and we go back to Smith Street to clean for him each Saturday. Mother does his washing and sees that he goes home with a couple of cold chops, some slices off the Sunday joint or a jar of home-potted meat.

Thelma, especially, looks forward to Granddad's Sunday visits when they walk up to Close's farm where the housing scheme ends at present and there are still country lanes. Thelma, my sister, is twelve going on thirteen and likes to do grown-up things like baking and gardening.

As I look out on the back garden, except that it is bordered off by the fence, it still looks as if it was part of the field beyond. I think the council turned it over for us and laid the concrete paths, but when it rains all the mud treads into the house. Granddad says that Thelma can help him rake it and sieve it through a riddle as preparation for sowing the grass seed.

This is a much smaller house than 86 Smith Street, where there were three flights of stairs not counting the steps that led from the kitchen-living room to the shop, nor the flight that went down to the cellar where Mother did her washing with her home-made soap. Here, when you open the front door and stand on the three-foot square of tiled floor, you can go directly up the stairs or open a door to go into the single living room, overcrowded by my mother's prized sideboard, our rosewood piano, (the only thing we ever bought on the "never never"), a gate-legged table, four straight chairs and two basket easy chairs. Beyond this room is a back-kitchen with a walled off space for the bath.

At Smith Street, Mother seemed to have time to chat for a couple of hours with Nurse MacKinlay who had popped in daily since we were babies. Some days Mother even found time to meet us from school and take us on a tram to Seaforth Sands or across the Mersey to New Brighton. From time to time she says, "I thought a small house would mean less housework but I'm beginning to wonder if I wasn't better off at Smith Street. When everyone is practically walking into the living room straight from the street and the mud treads right into the back kitchen, I'm never done washing two floors. It's true I haven't got that huge

4

grate to blacklead every morning but I miss the big coal oven. My dinners just don't taste the same any more."

We no longer have to rely on carrying hot water from the two iron kettles that stood on the hob all day at Smith Street. Here the hot water comes through the taps and it is a boiler at the back of the fireplace which heats it. Even on the hottest day we have to light a fire and there's no escaping to the big upstairs sitting room because here there is no sitting room.

At Smith Street, if we all returned to the house after dark we stood waiting in the doorway while Granddad used matches to light the gas mantle which hung from the ceiling. Here we just press a wall switch and the electric light comes on. I think Mother is saving up to buy lampshades because in the upstairs rooms only the naked bulbs hang down.

When we lived with Granddad, he was always giving Mother a couple of pounds to tide her over as he said "till Gerald gets home" and Granddad paid the largest share of the rent and rates and coal. I think Mother is struggling to find the seven (shillings) and sixpence rent for this house, and when doing the housework she doesn't sing as often as she used to. In the past she would frequently say "Smith Street gets me down", but when we lived there the number 3 tram stopped outside the shop and in ten minutes she was in Owen Owens, where for one (shilling) and ninepence she could buy a new hat and come home happy. Here the nearest tram at Dovecot is a twenty minute walk away and takes over half an hour to get to town so she gets "down" more often.

When she does the washing now she has to work in the back-kitchen. There's a boiler and a ringer so the clothes get lifted from the boiler to get rinsed in the sink and then they are put through the ringer. The old zinc bath that was used when we got our Saturday baths in front of the fire is put under the wringer to catch the water, but the water splashes and spills over the edges and the kitchen is awash. Mother has to mop up the floor and wait until it dries before she can use the gas rings to make a meal. She says, "I never thought I'd live to see the day when I'd have to admit that I miss the cellar." If it rains on washday, the clothes have to hang on the pulley above the gas-rings and they pick up all the cooking smells.

Come to think of it, I don't think we've had a hot dinner on a washday since we've lived here. I don't miss the scouse which was the usual washday dinner. It takes less time to eat a sandwich or a pie and tomato than it does to eat a knife and fork meal. There's less washing up and more time to play. We have had some very hot weather lately and we have to keep the back door open. The butter, kept in the back-kitchen, stands in a bowl of cold water to stop it melting, and the jug or opened bottle of milk is covered with a little bead-trimmed mesh doily to keep it free from dust and flies. There's a horrid sticky fly-paper hanging from the ceiling and some of the flies are still twitching. The meat is kept in a meat-safe which is a kind of cupboard with a wire front to let the air in. If there's thunder about, the milk goes off and we have to use tins of condensed milk which all Liverpool children call "Connyonny".

At Smith Street we were not allowed to play outside the shop. I'm not sure whether that was because, with the tram sheds opposite and four roads converging at "the lamp", there was too much traffic or because my mother feared we might learn to pick our noses and imitate the bad speech of the bare-footed children who stood around at the corner. We were allowed to go to the local parks and on the Mersey ferry with the Hunt girls who were older than us. Mrs. Hunt kept the draper's shop on Westminster Road which we passed on our walk to school. It was a long walk to school and Thelma and I came home every day for our midday dinner, so we walked it four times a day. I have already forgotten the names of some of the shops we passed but I remember that we had favourite songs that we sang as we walked along:

"The sun shines bright on Charlie Chaplin, his boots are cracklin' . . ."

"Amy! Wonderful Amy! You're the only girl that I adore . . ." (This because the headlines of every daily newspaper brought us news of Amy Johnson.)

That same year the newspapers followed the trial of a Doctor Ruxton who was accused of murdering his wife and wrapping her body in a carpet. I can't remember the words now but we sang another song about that as well.

Hunt's was where we bought our socks and gloves, and Mrs Hunt and Mother were great friends. Mother's best friend was Nurse MacKinlay who lived two doors away and, when she wasn't being a midwife, helped her brother, Ernie Sharp, serve in his grocery shop. Here Mother talks to Mrs. Sandeman next door and to Mrs. Whitely a few doors away but no-one replaces Nurse MacKinlay. Sometimes she lends a shilling to Mrs Eliot or Mrs Sweeney so that they can get their shoes back from the pawn-shop. They always return the shilling so that they can borrow it again if they are short the following week. Mother says, "It's little enough if it helps them out for God only knows how they manage with ten children in each family."

Today it is raining so I can't go out to play. On rainy days in Smith Street, Thelma and I used to set up toy shops or stoves to play all day long in the big upstairs sitting room where the windows looked out on the tramsheds. We didn't have to clear the toys away because, except for Sunday teas, we ate our meals downstairs in the kitchen. I haven't seen these toys since we moved here. I expect they are still in the packing cases which brought them because there are no spare cupboards to house them.

Even when we weren't playing with the shops or stoves, Thelma and I played together pretending to be mannequins or Roundheads and Cavaliers. Thelma is

8

too grown up to play with me now. She is probably in her room reading a "Secrets" magazine which she hides in the bottom of the wardrobe. We have to share the wardrobe and she was angry when I found the magazines. The stories in them have titles like "The House of Shame" and there's a picture on the cover of a baby in a shawl on a doorstep.

I said, "Can I read them when you've finished?"

Thelma, in her bossiest voice, said, "Of course you can't. They are grown-up magazines. You have to be at least twelve to understand them."

Thelma has always been bossy but she is getting worse lately. She is three years older than me and says that is why I have to do what she tells me. I think she got too much fuss made of her when we lived at Smith Street. She had long spells of illness, mostly rheumatic fever which left her with a weak heart, and she only had to ask for something to get it. I didn't mind this too much when she was ill as I usually shared any treat that was arranged for her. Also, I became much more important when I was sent on my own to get the pilot loaf from the corner shop or had to remember to collect shopping on my way home from school and bring home the right change. My new shiny patent leather shoes stayed un-scuffed and un-creased much longer because Thelma wasn't insisting that we play at trying to tread on one another's toes.

The only things Thelma and I do together now are to carry home the shopping from Dovecot shops and do the washing-up. We quarrel most when we have to do the washing-up. She says that as she is the eldest she should be the one to do the washing of the dishes, which means I have to dry and put away. She always finishes her job first and walks away and leaves me still doing my job. Often she is deliberately slow lifting the cups and plates from the water on to the draining board so I'm kept waiting, and when I think there is nothing left to dry she suddenly lifts all the cutlery from the bowl and tips out the water. It's not fair and I say so and she pulls a long face to make fun of me, and it's hard not to cry even though I know that will make her call me a cry-baby. We are shouting at one another when Mother appears from nowhere with the hairbrush and, with a swipe in each direction, says to Thelma, "Right, that's what you get for behaving like a bully," and to me, "And the same for you for behaving like a baby."

"It was all your fault," Thelma says as Mother retreats. "I hope you're pleased with yourself," and the bickering continues.

Thelma makes it very difficult for me to keep my resolution to be good. We were still at Smith Street and it was long after New Year when I made this resolution. Auntie Polly with the whiskery chin, together with her daughter, Cousin Nan, and *her* husband, Sidney Hughes, came for supper and cards most Saturday nights. Mother always baked meat pies and fruit tarts and these would sit cooling in the back-kitchen as, after our weekly baths, Thelma and I were getting ready for bed. One Saturday Mother had gone into Nurse MacKinlays for the five minutes which was usually half an hour, so Thelma and I thought she wouldn't notice if we broke off bits of the crispy edging on the pies so that we got a little taste. Mother was very angry with us and said that, because we had been stealing, we would be treated like prisoners and have to live on bread and water for a week. When we cried and pleaded with her to change her mind, she relented and said in that case there would have to be an alternative punishment. I wasn't there to see how Thelma was punished because I was told, "Go upstairs and take your knickers down. I'll be up right behind you to give you the smacked bottom you deserve." I really resented being treated like a baby when I was nearly ten years old and I determined there and then that never again would I subject myself to such an indignity.

It is raining again today and I think even though it is summer it is going to rain all day. If we still lived at Smith Street, I would be at Spellow Lane school but we left before they broke up for the summer holiday. No schools have yet been built on this housing estate so there is none to go to, which is great when we can play outside on the sunny days but not much fun when we are indoors.

The library is a long walk away at Dovecot and we haven't joined yet so I'll just have to find my Christmas *Schoolgirl Annual* and read the pages that I've skipped so far. I'm not looking forward to doing that because these are pages with recipes for making fudge or a knitting pattern for a school scarf and I don't much enjoy doing useful things.

If Mother was around I could ask her where she put the jigsaws, but she has gone for a lie-down on the bed, "just to rest her legs". She does this quite often and I think it is because she is getting old. She had her fortieth birthday in Smith Street over a month ago. While she is lying on the bed she writes a letter to Daddy who has not been home since we moved house. It will get sent to Hong Kong or Singapore, or somewhere else along the Suez canal route which takes him to China and Japan and lasts about three months. Before Mother posts it, she will have left an empty page for me to add my letter to him. When he writes to us I will get a page of his letter. It will say things like "So you went back to Smith Street last Saturday" or "I'm glad to hear you are doing the shopping for your mother", and I recognise all my own sentences just twisted round. I suppose our letters are not very exciting for him to read. We used to be able to write and tell him that we had been to town with Mother and had tea and toasted buns in Francis's cafe in Clayton Square or that Granddad had taken us on our regular Sunday trip to the Pier Head, but since we've lived here we don't get these outings any more. I used to think we were very rich but I'm not so sure of this any more.

Granddad tells Mother that there's still money coming in the till, thank God, but there's not enough business to keep three men working in the shop. He says it's hard to compete with big stores like Lewis's where you can leave your shoes at a counter and get them back an hour later. Granddad says, "What kind of

12

a sticking plaster job can anyone do in that short space of time? The men who are employed there have never been trained as shoemakers. They don't know one end of a shoe from the other — cobblers, the lot of them!" He tells us that, although he can only afford to pay Jack Fletcher or Mr Mann the odd day in the week to work for him, he is not often on his own in the shop because his friend Davey has been laid off and comes in most days to have a chat.

Granddad still buys most of his groceries from Ernie Sharp and his odd bit of cheese or boiled ham from Hannah's opposite. The butcher boy from Harriman's still calls and delivers a couple of times a week. Granddad and Davey often share an evening bottle of Bass and can choose between the Garrick and the Doric cinemas to take themselves to the pictures.

Granddad is a bit concerned that Thelma and I are missing out on over a month's schooling. He left school and ran away from home when he was twelve and he knows what he forfeited by so doing. He says, "Never mind. You are practically living in the country here and that's a whole lot better for your well-being than breathing in the dust of Smith Street."

I will have my tenth birthday at the end of August. Mother says it's a bit pointless asking Cousin Nan to make a summer dress when by then the summer will be nearly over and by this time next year I will have grown out of it. She says we still have to give Cousin Nan some sewing jobs to do because her husband hasn't had a job for years and there's no sign of him getting one in these bad times. She says, "Thelma's last gym slip will fit you when you start school after the summer, so I'll tell Cousin Nan to make you a Sunday winter dress for your birthday and you'll probably need a new pair of shoes, too, by then."

Because Thelma has the wardrobe in her bedroom, in mine under the window I have the desk which Uncle Sid made for us. It has been varnished but Mother says as usual he has spoiled the ship for a ha'porth o' tar. He should have spent longer sanding it down and he should have given it a second coat of varnish. It is a bit rough to the touch and there are patches that the varnish missed where little splinters of wood peel off. As I've got nothing else much to do on this wet day, I open the drawers in the desk to find the school books I had at Spellow Lane. We were allowed to keep the books because we had paid for them ourselves, as we also did for the jotters and the pens and even the nibs. This was because we paid fees to go there. Granddad helped find the school fees because the mother and two daughters who ran the school were related to the Sharps who were his customers, and when you are a shopkeeper you have to patronise your neighbouring shopkeepers.

In the drawers I find *Nature Myths* which I suppose I could read again for the fourth time. Another book is called *Greek and Norse Legends* so I know all about Pandora's box and Persephone and Ceres and Pluto and Thor and Loki. There's an atlas and a Wheaton's geography book, mostly maps showing temperature, rainfall, physical features and natural vegetation. The teacher used to dictate whole paragraphs from another

14

geography book for us to write in our jotters so that when parents visited the school they could see how advanced we were. Here is the Longman's French reader, all about Charles and Marie who always seemed to be telling one another about their pens or their pencils. We took turns reading it round the class aloud, pronouncing it exactly as if it were English. Here is the *Algebra for Beginners*, which made little sense to any of us but served to back up the prospectus of what was grandly called Westminster High School which boasted that French and Algebra were taught from the age of eight years.

I even find a pencil and a jotter with several unused pages so, because with my new low windowsill that I can sit on I see myself as Jo in Little Women, I could perhaps start writing the stories which are going to make me famous when I grow up. So far, the only long pieces I have written are the weekly compositions for school homework such as "The Autobiography of a Penny" and the one which earned me a certificate from the R.S.P.C.A. when at Mother's suggestion I wrote about how I felt as the hunted fox. The only foxes I have ever seen are in a picture book or at the museum where Granddad took us on wet Wednesday afternoons. On the other hand I have been able to make up rhymes for quite some time. I call them poems, and when one of them was printed in the Children's Corner of the *Liverpool Echo* I received a postal order for half a crown. Mother asked me how I wanted to spend the half-crown and, as it wasn't enough to buy a toy sewing machine or a toy typewriter, she suggested that I should spend sixpence of it and put the rest in the bank to save towards the toys I really wanted. I still have the same two shillings in the bank but I spent the sixpence on some pretty hair ribbons. Mother has finally agreed that I may let my hair grow long like Thelma's who, until recently, had ringlets. Her hair was wound round strips of rag when it was washed and often re-wound before she went to bed. She has two long plaits now which reach to her waist.

Mother says, "Having long hair is more trouble than it's worth, as you will find out when you have to wash it and comb out all the tangles and wind it round rags yourself. When you are nearly ten years old it won't be me that's doing it for you."

Thelma says long hair is a menace and the very day she leaves school she is going to have her plaits cut off. She says she will be able to please herself then because she will be earning her own money. She hates school except for the cookery lessons, and she wants to learn to be a baker. She is always persuading Mother to let her try her hand at making toffee or coconut ice and if she is in a good mood she gives me a bagful all to myself. It's not all bad having a big sister.

Summer 1934

There are a great many advantages to living at 95 Southdean Road. I am allowed to play outside in the

16

square with neighbouring children. No school has yet been built so there's a succession of long summer days in which I eventually learn to skip and bounce a ball against a wall saying, "One, two, three, Alera!" and a variety of other accompanying rhymes.

For the first time I am playing street games;

> The farmer wants a wife
> The farmer wants a wife
> Ee Ay Addio
> The farmer wants a wife.

This verse is followed by a string of others where the wife wants a child, the child wants a dog, the dog wants a bone and, finally, we all beat the bone. Each verse is rounded off with the chorus of "Ee Ay Addio". As a child is chosen, he or she stands in the centre of the circle while the others join hands and move round as they sing.

A similar singing game starts:

> In the garden stands a lady
> All she wants is a nice young man.

At the back of our house is a field leading into woods. We make tree houses and pretend we are people in the Hiawatha story. *Hiawatha* is a long poem we read at Spellow Lane. Throughout the summer, which is very hot, I play in just a summer dress and knickers.

Various people have been out to see us: Miss Blair, the teacher from Spellow Lane, Nurse McKinlay,

Auntie Polly, Alf and Georgina, and Nan and Sid. Most of them come only once. When they discover the long walk from the tram and the same distance to walk on their way back, they are not keen to visit a second time.

When these visitors arrive unexpectedly, and they usually do, in order to have something to offer them for tea, Thelma and I have to walk all the way to the Dovecot shops to buy the boiled ham, lettuce and tomatoes. When we get home we then have to trail up to Close's Farm for the extra milk.

I have my tenth birthday at the new house. I think I receive a dress as a present because I am growing out of all my summer dresses and Mother says they are too short. She lets me wear them for playing outside.

"Anything's good enough for that," she says, and I'm pleased because they are well up above my knees and I think that is why I can now skip and race around as fast as the other children.

All too soon it is the middle of September. Mother decides that, with no local school, we have to find one that Thelma and I can reach by tram. She either writes to the headmistresses or makes preliminary visits to the junior school in Boaler Street and the senior school in Shield Road.

The morning that we are to start at the new schools, Mother accompanies us to the Casino cinema in Kensington. This, she tells us, is the place where Thelma and I must meet at four o'clock in order to come home together.

18

My first day at Boaler Street is a bit of a culture shock. I'm unprepared for a class of fifty girls, eight of whom are called Joan. The teacher shouts all the time. To ensure the attention she requires, she addresses each pupil by her full name. I jump every time one of the Joans is called. I jump for most of the day.

It is very different from Spellow Lane. We all chant multiplication tables with Miss Bell constantly halting us momentarily as her pointer lands on a desk. This indicates to the pupil seated at the desk that it is her turn to continue the table, solo, until at the appropriate gesture from the teacher we all once again resume the refrain.

Sums are worked on the blackboard with an accompanying chorus: "Eight from seven I can't, add a ten. Eight from ten is two and seven is nine. Did I add a ten to the top line? Yes. So I must add a ten to the bottom line. Five and one are six. Six from four I can't", and so on. I find it all very baffling but I pick up clues from my fellow classmates.

Twelve o'clock comes and pupils who have brought sandwiches sit in a spare classroom. Here, I talk to a girl in my class who says she also travels on a number 10 tram and she will walk me up the road at four o'clock.

When school is over we walk to the tram stop outside the Casino cinema where Mother had said I was to meet Thelma. I am so busy chatting to my new-found friend that I forget about waiting for Thelma. It is only after we have been riding on the tram for a while and we reach the stop where my friend alights that I look out of the window as I am waving her off. I see the bigger shops and several cinemas and the traffic getting heavier. At last I realise that this tram is taking me into instead of out of the town centre. I tell the tram conductor. He is a kind man who appreciates my plight.

"If I was to let youse off 'ere, luv, you'd still be standing 'ere an 'our from now. Youse best stay put till we get to the Pier 'ead when we turn round again."

So I reach home about six o'clock.

"Heavens above," says my mother. "Ten minutes more and I'd have had the police looking for you." After I've told my tale, "Well, wonders will never cease. I'd have thought you had enough sense to cross the road to get the tram home. Still, I don't imagine you'll make that mistake again in a hurry."

From time to time through the school day Miss Monteith, the headmistress, appears in the classroom. It is the signal for the whole class to rise to its feet with "Good morning, Miss Monteith". I fear Miss Bell but Miss Monteith terrorises me. Once a week, after the morning playtime, she takes over for the music lesson. She appears followed by a procession of pupils carrying drums, cymbals, tambourines and other percussion instruments, which they distribute among the class. I am well pleased that I have been given a drum. A blackboard is pushed into the classroom. It is covered with rows of chalked circles, crosses, triangles, etc. With Miss Monteith directing us, we begin to play our instruments. I'm enjoying this but Miss Monteith rattles her pointer on the desk for us to come to a halt.

She insists that some pupil is not paying attention to the blackboard and we begin again. I watch the other drummers warily so that I am keeping in time with them but I am usually a couple of beats behind. Miss Monteith grows crosser and crosser. It is obvious that the blackboard is meant to guide us but none of it makes sense to me. Happily for me the lesson comes to an end without her discovering my short-comings, so the next music lesson is likely to be just as big a fiasco.

I go home and describe the lesson to my mother who laughs until the tears run down her cheeks. Each night I relate the happenings of the school day and the attention I receive makes me feel as I did when I stood on top of the desk to say my poem at the Spellow Lane party. I spend my day at school, an alien, hardly daring to breathe lest I incur the teacher's wrath. When I am safely home, in familiar surroundings with my mother as audience, I can manage to realise that the events of the day are ludicrous.

Each Saturday we go down to Granddad's. Mother cleans and cooks all day and Thelma and I are set tasks such as polishing the furniture and cleaning the silver. Cleaning the silver is a hateful job. A paste made of Goddard's plate powder mixed with methylated spirits is applied to each spoon or fork in turn. The revolting smell fills the whole room. As the paste dries and turns black, it has to be polished off with another cloth. Thelma and I have an argument about who "puts on" and who polishes. We work at the kitchen table covered with old newspapers. I make the work less tedious by reading the picture strip advertisements for Mansion Polish and Brasso. I like any form of reading matter where the people speak into balloons much as they do in comics. I used to enjoy the series of pictures in the annuals that told the stories of Bobby Bear and Pip, Squeak and Wilfred, which is a long time ago before I could read.

When we finish our chores there's not much to do at Smith Street, so I root in the dresser drawers for old magazines. I find a whole series of children's books of knowledge. The articles in them do not enthral me but on the back page of each issue is a puzzle page. By dint of looking ahead at the answers I manage to teach myself how to do acrostics and laddergrams. There are also two heavy leather-bound books of information. I think they were prizes that Granddad won at school. One is called *Famous Men and Women* and the other *Tales of the British Empire*. In the centre of the second one is a double page of the flags of all the nations, in colour. In these books I read about Florence Nightingale, Grace Darling, Captain Cook and Scott of the Antarctic.

I go to Hannah's to get a packet of Granola biscuits for Granddad. He keeps the packet in a black-lacquered tea caddy with a flower design on it in colours. It is one that Daddy brought home from Japan and the packet fits exactly inside it. It sits on the mantlepiece. Pinned on to the wallpapered kitchen walls with drawing pins Granddad has various coloured pictures of flowers. They are given away with each new copy of the gardening magazine that he buys, now that

22

he is regularly buying plants for our new garden. After dinner each Sunday he and Thelma walk round to Close's farm and come back laden with geraniums, lobelias, alyssums, antirrhinums and calceolarias. Thelma helps plant them in the garden. They have also bought an elderberry bush with black berries and another with red berries called cotoneaster. We all pronounce it "Cotton Easter".

It is between four and five o'clock when we leave Smith Street. We take the tram to the Majestic cinema at the junction of Moss Street and Low Hill. We go into the sweet shop where Mother buys chocolate coconut caramels. In the cinema she produces big, green, sour apples. We eat these as we watch George Raft in a gangster film and Hopalong Cassidy in a cowboy adventure. In every Hopalong film I've ever seen the gunshots come from behind the same boulder.

It is dark and often damp when we come out of the cinema to take the tram home. After walking from the tram stop, we reach home cold and tired. Mother says it's not worth lighting a fire so she makes hot Bournvita and we eat Ovaltine rusks round the gas fire in her bedroom until bedtime.

Mother says that if we come home from school one day and there's no-one in, then we have to go two doors up to Mrs. Whitely. She has a daughter called Dorothy who is the same age as me. Mr. Whitely, like my Daddy, goes to sea except he works for the White Star line. He only goes across the Atlantic to America and gets home every three weeks. We are all great friends. Dorothy and

I have joined the Ovaltineys so we signal to each other with torches after the lights are out at night and we write notes in invisible ink or in secret codes. We sing the Ovaltiney song.

Mother says that one day soon she will need to go to the hospital to collect the new baby and that's why she could be late getting home. I tell Thelma that this is not the whole truth. I'm pretty sure the baby comes out of its mummy's tummy.

"Where did you hear that?" Thelma asks.

"Well, I didn't exactly hear it. At school Miss Bell draws a flower on the blackboard. It's a sort of cut-down-the-middle flower so that you can see inside it. She labels the petals, the sepals, the stamens, the anthers, and the pistil at the top of the seed box. She shows us how the bee carries the pollen from one flower to another to make the seeds grow. Then she talks about cats having kittens and dogs having puppies. I've just put two and two together and I think babies are born in the same way."

"Well," says Thelma, "Mother has a big tummy so perhaps the baby is inside it."

We come home on the 26th of November and it's Mrs. Whitely who opens the door. "Your Mummy's in bed not well," she says. "You can have your tea in my house."

When at last we see the baby, it is a little boy and Mother says he is going to be christened John Francis but we can call him Frank.

Next day I go to school and tell the girls that I have a new baby brother. "Congratulations," says a girl

24

called Beryl who crosses the playground to shake hands with me. I am very surprised. Beryl has gone out of her way to ignore me since my composition was read out to the class along with hers.

There is no church near the new housing scheme so we are going to have baby Frank christened at St Athanasius, near Smith Street.

It is the Sunday before Christmas when we go back to Granddad's. We attend an afternoon carol service and, after it is over, we stand round the font at the back of the church and the vicar sprinkles water on Frank's head and gives him his names. Frank wears the long christening robe that Thelma and I wore as babies when we were baptised. It is made of very fine lawn with a high neck and long sleeves ending in tiny cuffs. The bodice and hem have rows of narrow tucks that are hand-sewn. Our new baby cries all through the service so it is not easy to hear the words that the vicar is saying.

At last we go back to Smith Street where Granddad has the table laid and we drink ginger wine and eat Crawfords Tartan shortbread. We raise our glasses and toast the health of the new baby. Christmas has begun in advance this year.

In reality, Christmas comes and goes this year like no other Christmas that I can remember. I already have a baby doll that I call Peggy. Mother makes her look new by dressing her in a new outfit that she has knitted. Beside her on Christmas morning there is a doll-sized dummy and feeding bottle so that I can pretend she is a real baby.

Mother is unwell in bed with the new baby most of Christmas Day. Auntie Polly comes with Granddad to see us but there's no Christmas dinner and there's neither Christmas tree nor decorations.

I'm not sure but I think we are quite poor now. Mother has to buy Cow and Gate baby food for Frank because when she was breast-feeding him, he wasn't getting enough nourishment and that was why he cried day and night. One of our new neighbours reported us to the Cruelty to Children people who came to the house. Mother said that was all right because the baby screamed all the time they were here. So, after that, Mother starts to take Frank to the mother and baby clinic at the tramstop at Dovecote. She misses not having Nurse McKinlay to help her look after this baby.

By January some shops have been built and one by one they are opening. They are only five minutes walk away. More significantly for us two new schools have been erected within walking distance.

"Not before time," Mother says. "Most of the children in this housing scheme have run wild for nigh on two years." She decides that there is no point in us continuing to go to Boaler Street and Shield Road schools through the winter and, as soon as they are opened, we can go to the new schools. She has only one regret. She paid for the material for Thelma to make a nightdress in her school sewing lessons and now it looks as if that money is going to be wasted.

Thelma tells me it was a disaster in any case. She hates sewing.

I am in the top class of the new school where Miss Gore is the headmistress. She is probably in her fifties, very tall and straight, good-looking in a severe kind of way with high colour, horn-rimmed spectacles and cropped, silvery-white hair.

We have the desks and the blackboards but we are still waiting for all the books and equipment to arrive. All our lessons are oral. A spelling lesson is taken by a student who has each member of the entire class in turn spelling out aloud words such as "receive" and "deceive". I hear the wrong spelling so many times that when my turn comes round I too am wrong and I'm mortified.

Our teacher, Miss Banks, has us chanting the two times table. I am the only girl in the class who knows anything beyond the two times table. I know too much and Miss Banks would gladly be rid of me. Her opportunity presents itself when Miss Gore appears in the classroom and asks that one girl be appointed as headmistress's monitress. Miss Banks selects me. From then on, if Miss Gore's bell rings I have to leave the classroom and get myself, post-haste, down to Miss Gore's room at the opposite end of the long corridor.

The stock begins to arrive and my first job is to distribute the new registers. I am given a stiff-backed book in which I will collect the attendance totals from the various classrooms twice a day. The teachers ask me to check their totals by counting the pupils. I collect the registers each morning and re-collect them from the teachers in the afternoon. Miss Gore counts out pencils, pens, exercise books, rulers, rubbers and chalk for each class. I run up and down the corridor delivering them. The text books begin to arrive and they are counted out and allocated. Everything is new. All the teachers know I am Miss Gore's special helper and so, just before twelve o'clock, I am allowed out of school to purchase from the local shops the items they require for their midday snacks.

Miss Gore presides over a daily assembly in the hall. Miss Banks and Miss Hosendoff take it in turns to play the piano but after the first hymn and prayer the other teachers leave to go to their classrooms where they have so much to organise. We stay for another half-hour with Miss Gore who, with the help of words written up on a blackboard, teaches us the words of the hymns that she expects us to memorise. We sing

Holy, Holy, Holy, Lord God Almighty,
Early in the morning our song shall rise to thee.

and

Daisies are our silver, buttercups our gold,
These are all the treasure we can have or hold.

and

Summer suns are glowing over land and sea

28

Mother with her very cross baby says it's her clinic day today and she can't get back from Dovecote for twelve o'clock. She gives us sixpence each and says, "Buy something to eat from the shops on your way home."

She never asks us how we spend the money so we buy three cream cakes each. It is synthetic cream and it doesn't taste like the cream in the cakes from Reeces and Sayers, but Thelma and I enjoy sampling things which normally we wouldn't be allowed to buy.

As the days grow longer and milder, Mother is waiting at the door for us at four o'clock. She takes Thelma inside to help her clean the house which she hasn't had time to do all day because the baby takes up so much of her time. This house has no hall, just a tiled square to stand on between the foot of the stairs and the door that leads into the one overcrowded living room which now also accommodates the pram. Across this square she drags the pram outside and says, "Two hours, Joan. You walk the pram and I'll be all done in two hours."

I'm glad it's not me helping with the housework. I push the pram to the shops and there I buy gobstoppers. You get five for a penny and they last a long time. It is interesting to keep taking the gobstopper out of one's mouth and counting how many times it changes colour. Sometimes I choose Cupid's Lips, little hard red jellies in the shape of crescents. The red dye comes out on the tongue. Occasionally I buy Sticky Lice. This comes in the form of twigs that you can suck forever. Frank goes to sleep so I push the pram up past Close's farm, and when I am safely away from all the houses I sit in a lane and read my book until it is time to go home. Peter, the man who delivers our milk, tells my mother that I'm deep in a book and anything could be happening to the baby. Mother repeats this to me.

"Is that true?" she demands.

"I only read when he's asleep," I say.

She sighs, "God knows there's not much in the way of a treat for you these days."

Because I am very conscious of my own importance, I tell my mother how I spend most of my days at school. She is horrified.

She goes to school to see the headmistress. She tells Miss Gore that she doesn't send her daughter to school to run messages all day long, and how is Joan supposed to perform in the Junior City Scholarship examination in March when she is getting no education. She is not one of the parents who let her children run wild when there was no school in this area. She paid tram fares to send them to school.

Miss Gore doesn't come across a parent like my mother every day and for a moment even she is at a bit of a loss for words.

"Mrs. Lowe," she says, "do you realise that I am in the position of starting this school from scratch with pupils most of whom have not attended school for two years? They have forgotten everything they ever knew. All the teachers in the school have their work cut out trying to bring their classes up to standard and, not least, Miss Banks with the top class who are having to learn how to add and subtract all over again."

"My daughter can do fractions and decimals," boasts my mother.

"Well, there's no way Miss Banks will have time to teach your daughter separately, Mrs. Lowe."

"What, then, do you propose to do about it?" persists my mother, holding her ground.

"Well," says Miss Gore, "she's likely to be the only pupil from this school being entered for the secondary school qualifying examination this March and it is now February, so what I'll do is this. She can wait at my door every morning after assembly and I'll give her the first half-hour of my own time. I will set work for her to do each night at home under your supervision and I will correct it the following day."

A truce has been reached. I remain the headmistress's monitress, I continue to do my morning and afternoon register duties, and Miss Gore spends part of her day setting and correcting my homework.

She opens one of the new reading books at a coloured illustration and asks me to describe what I see in the picture. When I am ready to write this description at home, it must include phrases such as "in the foreground" and "in the distance". Occasionally she asks me about the classics of English Literature. "What! Ten years old and never read *David Copperfield*?" She is appalled by my ignorance and that of the present world in general.

March arrives and I set off with pen, pencils, ruler and rubber for St Edmund's College to sit the examination. I have to travel on two buses and the journey takes over an hour. It is by no means the nearest high school but Miss Hosendoff is a former pupil and she, Miss Gore and my mother decided together that this was the best choice for me.

Part of the English test is "Look at the series of pictures below and use them to tell an original story."

I do not know what "original" means but it is quite clear to me that the characters arrayed in these particular costumes and in possession of caskets have stepped right out of the pages of *The Merchant of Venice* which, a short while age, we were reading at Spellow Lane. I write down as much of Shakespeare's story as I can in the time available.

A letter arrives to say I have failed the examination. There are no recriminations. I am only ten years old and I will have another chance next year.

Miss Gore continues to set work for me and has recommended to my mother that she buy me a weekly copy of the *Children's Newspaper* to keep me abreast of current events. The *Children's Newspaper* makes very dull reading so I turn to the back page with the Jacko cartoon and then cast it to one side. I feel guilty because it costs sixpence and, now that Granddad no longer lives with us, we do not have many sixpences to spare.

I resit the entrance examination in March 1936. I go back to school in the afternoon and, in front of the whole class, Miss Banks asks me about the question papers.

"Which of these compositions did you choose to write?"

"I did 'A Ride on a Magic Carpet'."

"Splendid!" she says, "Just the one I would have chosen. Where did you go?"

I'm puzzled. "I didn't go anywhere. I just cruised around."

"I don't believe it. All those wonderful lands I've talked about in Geography lessons. You could have gone to Canada or Japan but, no, you just cruised around. You can say goodbye to your chances of getting into a secondary school."

I go home and Mother says, "What did they ask you in the Current Affairs questions?"

"Oh, they asked us to name the two leaders in the Abyssinian War."

"Did you remember?"

"Oh, yes. I wrote down Mussolini and Addis Ababa."

"For Heaven's sake, child, that's the capital of Abyssinia. The ruler is Haile Selassie," and then, to that invisible audience she so frequently addressed, "This is ridiculous. This child doesn't even know things that are in the news every day. She doesn't know the difference between the name of a city and the name of a king. It's no use. If it's only for the sake of this child's education, we'll have to buy a wireless."

So I have provided the excuse for the acquisition of our first wireless set. We hurry home at lunch time to hear Henry Hall and his BBC dance orchestra. George Elrich sings all the novelty numbers like "Animal Crackers in my Soup", and when "Here's to the next time" indicates the end of the programme we join in with the vocalist. We race back home at four o'clock to listen to the Francis Durbridge serial. Until now I have never heard wireless programmes except for once at Smith Street, when Mrs. Lapin lent us her cat's whisker set to listen to Children's Hour. I was very little then and I was listening through earphones when a voice said, "Hello, children. This is Auntie Muriel speaking." I rushed to find Mummy and tell her that our Auntie Muriel was on the wireless.

Despite the fears of Miss Banks and my mother, I receive a letter to say I have been successful in the junior city scholarship. Miss Gore is delighted. I am her star pupil. I am the feather in her cap in her opening year at this school. She announces the news at assembly and I am clapped and cheered. I am taken into every classroom and the children are told, "Joan Lowe is the first scholarship pupil in this school." I am even paraded round all the classes in the boys' department. There I meet a boy named Eric Williams. He is also taking his bow in front of the classes for he is the first boy in the school to win a scholarship. I think I am perhaps the only girl in the school whose name is known to every pupil.

Before I leave that summer we hold our first sports day in the school playground. I team up with the best runner in the class for the three-legged race. We have been practising every playtime and we win with yards to spare. We keep the same partners for the race where we start by standing at opposite ends of the playground. My partner races to me and gives me the sum to which I have to work out the answer so that she can run back with it to the finishing line. We are very confident. As I start to wrestle with the figures, the playground is one big chant of "Joan Lowe, Joan Lowe, Joan Lowe". It is too much for me. I cannot concentrate on the addition as my head swells, remembering all the schoolgirls' annuals that I have ever read. This is not fiction. It is all my dreams come true. I am the most popular girl in the school. With all these distracting thoughts it is little wonder that I am slow totting up the figures. It is my partner with her fleetness of foot who saves us from humiliation.

As we break up for the summer holiday, we celebrate the Silver Jubilee of King George V and Queen Mary. All the Liverpool schoolchildren receive commemorative silver-coloured tins with the sovereigns' heads in colour on the front. They are to be used as pencil cases. I help to give them out to the classes. It is the last day of term and, finding there are about half a dozen of these little, flat tins excess to our needs, much to my surprise and pleasure Miss Gore gives them to me.

Frank is still a young baby when Granddad tells Mother one day that her own mother wants to come back to Smith Street.

"You need your head reading, Dad, even if you are only considering it."

"Now, now, Nan, she's an old woman. My guess is that the relatives she has been living with have turned her out. She's nowhere to go."

"Too bad!" sniffs my mother. "She's got some nerve wanting you to take her back after walking out on you over twenty years ago. I hope you are going to say no."

"Well, it's no use pretending I could live with her again because I couldn't and I've told her as much, but I said I'd ask you to have her."

"Dad, you didn't! I can't believe it. It's hard enough to manage without an interfering old woman who is stone deaf."

"I'd give you the money for her keep, Nan."

"I'm not talking about money. I'm talking about the fact that she's a born trouble-maker and I'm damned certain she hasn't changed for the better."

"She is your mother. She could be of help with the baby. I think you should give it a trial."

So the grandmother I had never seen before comes to live with us and Thelma and I have to share a bed again. It doesn't last long. Life between my mother and my grandmother is a continuous argument. They use sign language to talk to one another so most of the time we do not know what they are saying. In the final row my mother is shaking her little finger at her over and over again and shouting. "You're bad. Do you know what I am saying to you? You're a bad woman. You've got an evil mind."

Next day she tells Granddad, "She's got to go. I won't have her in the house any longer. Would you believe that woman is jealous of the fondness you show to Thelma. We'd all be better off if she were dead."

"Nan! That's a dreadful thing to say. Mark my words, you'll live to regret it."

Grandma has gone away and I don't know where she has gone, but one day my mother's wish comes true and we hear that Grandma has died. The funeral is to be from Smith Street and Granddad has made all the arrangements.

On the day of the funeral my mother wears a grim face for the whole of the day but at no time is it grimmer than when the hearse draws up outside the shop door and I hear her say, "Oh, for God's sake, Dad, it's 1936. Did it have to be horses?"

September 1936

I am wearing my new school gym slip and blazer and regulation grey felt hat. I carry my first school bag holding my pencil case and packed lunch, and a separate shoe bag with the house shoes into which I will change at school. The blazer is black with purple binding and on the second bus I see many girls who also wear purple in their uniforms. They all alight at Arundel Avenue so I do too, only to discover that I have made a mistake. This is the wrong stop for my school and I have to wait for the next bus. This puts me off at Prince's Park gates and I walk round the corner to Saint Edmund's College for Girls.

It is more like Spellow Lane school than Boaler Street or Colwell Road because it is a big converted house standing in its own grounds where there are steps leading down to gravel paths and well-trimmed lawns. In the classroom the names of the scholarship pupils are read out and we line up to collect our free text books. They are not new and we are told that they must be returned in good condition at the end of the year. Meanwhile they are to be taken home, and by the end of the week are to be covered in brown paper and labelled with name, class and subject. There are a number of fee-paying pupils in the class who pay for their new books. Subject teachers give out exercise books and we have big rough note books.

I revel in just looking at the pencil case which I was given as a present for passing the entrance examination. It is so much grander than the bulky wooden one I had at Spellow Lane which got scratched and stained with ink. My new pencil case is divided into three sections and, as well as pens, pencils, ruler and rubber, it has a geometry set. There is a little metal case for spare nibs and one whole section filled with coloured pencils. It folds up and fastens with a snap fastener.

We spend most of our first day writing out subject timetables so that we will know which days we must have the requisite books in school and which days to bring the gym blouse we must change into to wear over our navy blue gym knickers.

At the morning and afternoon intervals, not referred to in this school as playtimes, prefects appear with trays of Cadbury chocolate bars which they sell for a penny each. I am trying very hard not to look in any way different from the other girls but I have no money to buy a bar of chocolate.

It is well after five o'clock when I arrive home to recount the highlights of the day. When she hears about the chocolate Mother comes up with a solution.

"I'm giving you fivepence a day for fares, that's two (shillings) and a penny a week and that's a lot of money. If it wasn't for the five shillings a week that Thelma earns at the bakery I couldn't afford even that. It costs three ha'pence on the second bus because you get off near school. If you get off at the fare stage one stop before and walk back to that stage after school, you can have the penny that you save to buy a bar of chocolate. If your granddad were here he'd no doubt say you'll be walking off more than the penny in shoe leather but we'll forget about that."

Thelma is working in Field's Bakery because she could leave school after her fourteenth birthday which was in September. This meant she did not have to go back to school after the summer term finished in July. Thelma hated school so she wanted to leave and Mother took her down to Field's Bakery to be apprenticed and learn the trade. Thelma says she likes working there with about four other people and others that serve in the shop. I think she mostly greases the tins and washes the floor. She is frightened of the cockroaches. The staff think Mr. Fields is very mean because they have to pay for the individual steak pie or blackcurrant tart or bun that they eat. She says Scotty, who is responsible for making the bread and looking after the ovens, regularly and deliberately drops a cake on purpose. A broken cake cannot be sold in the shop so they each get a taste. Millie makes all the puff pastry and Molly does the cake-decorating. Thelma likes Molly best because she lets her watch so that she can come home and make fondant creams in different colours.

At the end of the first week I bring home a letter which tells mother that, as a scholarship pupil, I am entitled, together with the use of free books, to free bus tickets and two pounds a term towards school uniform. From now on, to get my daily bar of chocolate I must barter one of my bus tickets for a penny. When the day comes for the two pounds to be paid out, Mother meets me in town straight after school and, as a special treat, I am taken to Lewis's café for a Knickerbocker Glory. This is served in a tall glass with a long spoon to reach down through the whipped cream and the ice-cream to the fruit at the bottom.

I work very hard during my first year in secondary school and I conscientiously do my homework. I like most of the lessons but I am very scared in the arithmetic class as Miss Yates, small, grey-haired and irritable, fires mental arithmetic questions at us and expects an immediate answer. When it is my turn, my voice refuses to rise above a whisper and Miss Yates becomes impatient and fractious at the time it takes for some other pupil to relay to her the answer I am giving. I get good marks in the first report and I am top of the class in French, an achievement never to be repeated because in this term only I have the advantage of being acquainted with much of the vocabulary previously presented by "Charles and Marie" at Spellow Lane.

This is a Church of England school, so on Ascension Day we all walk in panama hats and blazers, whatever the weather, to the recently built cathedral. The service is over by lunchtime so we have a half-day's holiday.

There is a gym hall in this school. It is where we hold morning assembly when all but prefects and teachers sit cross-legged on the floor. There are wall bars, a vaulting box, a horse and benches for balancing exercises. I am not very good at any gym activities. The one time it is sheer enjoyment for me is on the last lesson of the term when we play Pirates. The benches and mats are strewn at intervals over the floor which represents the sea. Anything other than the floor is the ship. One child appointed as pirate pursues the rest as we shin up the wall bars, swing from the ropes or take wild leaps from one piece of apparatus to the next. If the pirate catches up with you, you drop out of the game because you are captured. If your feet touch a spot of uncovered floor you drop out because you are drowned. It is wonderful: it is exhilarating. We are allowed to scream and it has the same effect on me as the day we spent with the D'Arcy girls, racing round the empty swimming baths.

We have an annual speech day when parents are invited and we assemble in newly pressed gym slips (any spots having been previously home-cleaned with vinegar), freshly laundered blouses, newly washed hair and shiny faces in Saint George's Hall. We sing "Jerusalem" and "I Vow to thee my Country" and we all cheer when the chief speaker of the evening announces that we are to be given an extra day's holiday.

Outside of school, a memorable event of this year is the death of King George V. All the normal radio programmes are cancelled. We listen to the commentary that accompanies the cortège through the streets with a background of "Over the Sea to Skye", for this is the death of our sailor king. When this ends, the Dead March continues to be played for the rest of the day. We switch off the radio, but my father who happens to be home at the time persists in humming the tune in his extremely tuneless voice which I have inherited. He hums his way through the various chores of the day until my mother finally explodes with "For God's sake, Gerald, give it a rest."

During my next year at secondary school my attendance is not very good. One reason for this is that I am afflicted with a series of styes and boils. Each stye that I suffer is bigger and more painful than the last. When one appears on my top lid, my eye is virtually closed and I cannot open it when I wake up. When the lower lid has the infection, it is even more painful as the head of the stye not only obscures my vision but feels excruciating every time I blink. I experiment with an eye patch but despite this I cannot bear to sit in electric light. I bathe the eyes throughout the day in very hot water to dissolve the boracic powder which gives some temporary relief. I use Golden Eye ointment and even cold tea-leaves all to no avail.

"I cannot believe that you have to be absent from school just because you have a stye," says one teacher, and I have to explain that more often than not I have three styes at the same time and I cannot see to read or write. I repeat her words to my mother who then takes me to the doctor. I start a course of injections in the thigh. My whole leg swells up and hardens and becomes so stiff that I cannot walk. After a while the "cure" has to be abandoned. As the doctor admits, "No sense in keeping up a cure that's worse than the disease."

The worst boil is one which appears on my bottom. Mother applies hot poultices "to bring it to a head" and I sit in a chair from which the seat has been removed and the space padded with cushions to prevent me from falling through.

In the summer of 1938, just as I am about to celebrate my fourteenth birthday Thelma has a fall from her bike coming home from work.

When Thelma was fourteen she had a birthday party. Mother seemed to bake for days and she made Madeline cakes, sponge covered in jam and sprinkled with coconut, quite the fanciest cakes she had ever made. There was a birthday cake and special presents and a party to which Thelma invited her friends.

When my birthday arrives, my twin friends, Pat and Betty from Sunday School, give me a strawberry pink pinafore dress which, with guidance from their mother, they have made for me. It fits perfectly and with it I wear a lovely silk smocked peasant blouse which my father has brought from abroad. There is no party or cakes because Thelma is in bed ill, in and out of fits of delirium. The doctor is called to the house. The ambulance arrives to take her to Mill Road Hospital where her illness is diagnosed as septicaemia. Mother is to spend the next four months visiting Thelma in hospital. My sister is in a ward where my mother is allowed to visit at any time but no other visitors are allowed.

I think my mother writes to my headmistress to say she has no choice but to keep me from school to look after my little brother who is not yet four.

To me Mother says, "Thelma is seriously ill and it is possible that the police will come to the door to tell me that I have to go immediately to the hospital. This could happen in the middle of the night. Just keep Frank happy. I'm not asking you to look after the house, just play with him. You can do that, can't you?"

Of course I can do that. I may be fourteen and I don't play with toys any more, but I love building up his trolley-load of polished, natural-coloured wooden bricks and creating a miniature village from the smooth coloured shapes, representing trees and houses that make up the kit of Playskool. These are toys which my father has brought from abroad that do not exist in our shops.

Frank and I have Grand Prix races with his small racing cars and mock battles with his toy soldiers that we place on the battlements of his toy fort. We even have a miniature cannon to fire matchsticks which often end up striking the piano and leaving dents in it. I do the dusting so for a long time they escape Mother's notice.

Mother comes and goes to the hospital just long enough to show us the tasty morsel of chicken breast that she has bought, ready-cooked at Cooper's, to try to tempt Thelma's poor appetite. She takes in *Film Review* and *Picturegoer*, hoping that Thelma may be well enough to look at them.

Mother says, "Thelma is being given doses of M&B tablets to try to disperse the huge abscesses that have developed on her shoulder and at the base of her spine. They make her very sick. If these tablets don't work, the abscesses will have to be lanced. When I went in the ward today the screens were round two more beds; that means two more patients have died."

As Mother forecast, the police do call more than once and each time it is in the early hours of the morning. Granddad comes up each Wednesday and Sunday and tells me what a great help it is for my mother to have me.

It is December now and Mother suggests that I take Frank to Lewis's toy fair. "I don't have time to buy Christmas presents," she says. "You can choose something for Frank's present and you can spend half of the ten shillings I am giving you on a Christmas present for yourself."

The toy fair occupies a whole floor and Frank and I spend a day there. We watch the various demonstrations of Meccano and clockwork train sets. I buy him a small metal clockwork bubble car. I spend a long time watching a demonstration of a stencil set. I watch the different sheets of stencil being used to create scenes. I can neither draw nor paint but with this I can see myself becoming an artist, so I buy it for myself.

I look forward to Mother coming home with the film magazines that have been the rounds of the ward and now become mine. I look at the pictures of the Marx brothers, Betty Grable, Michael Denison, Dulcie Gray and Googie Withers. In bed at night I think about the film stars and the clothes they wear and imagine myself among them.

It is Christmas Eve and we are back at 86 Smith Street to make it easier for Mother to go back and forwards to the hospital over Christmas. She shows us the new dressing gown and slippers that are to be Thelma's Christmas presents. There is a chicken, trussed and ready to be cooked, that sits all day on the kitchen dresser. Frank looks at its legs sticking up in the air and after a long while says, "Why doesn't somebody tell it to sit down?" There are neither decorations nor a Christmas tree, and I feel this is very unfair to my little brother. I vow that from now on, whether anybody else bothers or not, I will be the person in our house who ensures that Christmas will be for him as it was for me when I was little.

One day in January Mother comes home having spent all night at the hospital.

"I think Thelma has come through the crisis," she says. "Under the anaesthetic in the operating room she sang 'Bread of Heaven' all the way through. They could hear her in the wards and in the corridors all over the hospital."

At the end of February Thelma is sent to a convalescent hospital in Southport and I return to school. There aren't many fine days to provide her with the fresh air to build up her strength, but in Southport there are many cinemas and with the pocket money Mother gives her she spends part of each day going to the pictures. She tells Mother she hates the hospital food so she buys extra food in the baker's shops. One day a bus trip is organised for the patients. It goes to Liverpool and she recognises Everton Valley, so she just leaves the bus and takes the tram home. She does not return to Southport. She has had some kind of sunray treatment so she now has a mass of frizzy hair like an African. She goes back to sing in the church choir each Sunday.

The church figures quite largely in our lives now. I suppose it was erected about two years ago and it doesn't look in the least like a church. It is a wooden hut with a cross on the roof and it is called Saint David's. It is at the top of King's Drive beside the Page Moss tram terminus in the more recently developed part of the housing scheme which was fields when we first moved house.

The curate-in-charge is plump and pink-faced and very jolly. His wife is black with frizzy hair like Thelma's. His grown-up sons are brown and one of them is very handsome. To encourage the attendance of young people, the curate has founded a group of Archers and Maids Marion. Adult leaders take the names of Robin Hood, Will Scarlet and the rest of the merry men. The leaders and all the members wear uniforms of Lincoln green with forage caps to match. They behave much as scouts and girl guides, parading on Sundays, meeting two or three times a week and camping at Sherwood forest.

I must be about the only girl of my age who is not a Maid Marion, but I tell my mother I have too much homework and between that and piano practice and the distance I have to travel to school I am left with no time to go to meetings. Mother does not persist. "It's all a bit of a farce" is her only comment.

Friar Tuck is brimming over with fund-raising ideas to enable us to build a proper church hall to replace the hut. He organises whist drives, beetle drives, mid-week socials and Saturday night film shows. With Pat and Betty, the twins, I attend some of the socials and film shows. There is a screen and a projector and we watch the old "silents" for the cost of twopence entrance fee. The real money is made from the shop, selling bottles of lemonade, lollipops, slabs of toffee and sweets of various kinds, bought in wholesale and making good profit. My mother is one of a group of voluntary workers who regularly clean the church so she now has friends. From time to time they voice their suspicions about "Robbing Hood", the name they playfully give to the leader of the whole money-making enterprise.

Pat and Betty are attending confirmation classes in Saint David's. I make the excuse that my school runs confirmation classes and I prefer to be confirmed with my school friends.

Each June we have a Rose Queen festival in the field surrounding the church. It is the biggest money-making event of the year. There are many side shows and stalls selling crisps, lemonade and ice-cream. The first year I, along with the twins, was a maid of honour to the Rose Queen. We paraded in long dresses, white satin shoes and wore floral head-dresses and elbow-length gloves. We had to attend rehearsals in order to practise walking in pairs in step behind the Rose Queen and perfecting a court curtsey. On the day of the fête we were driven round the housing scheme in a flower-decorated landau. All this had to be repeated the following year as retinue to the retiring queen. The whole event was covered by the *Liverpool Echo*.

It is Spring 1939 and we have to choose another Rose Queen and her retinue. At the close of Sunday School we are asked to write the names of our choice on pieces of paper, which are handed in and counted. I think our choice is restricted to senior girls. Mrs. West, the superintendent, appears after the count and announces that Joan Lowe has been elected as Rose Queen. It is only with hindsight that I realise this is a repetition of the "popularity" I enjoyed at my final sports day at Colwell Road. There is only one non-Catholic school in the district. Most of the children who voted for me knew my name when they didn't know or couldn't spell the names of my contenders.

Mother, Mrs. West and Friar Tuck's wife decide that I will be robed in ivory satin and a purple velvet train trimmed with imitation ermine. Paper dress-making patterns and materials are bought and Cousin Nan is resurrected to do the sewing. It is decided that Frank is angelic enough at four to be dressed in mauve satin and carry the crown on a purple velvet cushion. There is a photograph of me taken by a press photographer which appears not only in the *Liverpool Echo* but on cards produced in hundreds, heralding the date on which the ceremony will be carried out by the vigorous campaigner against capital punishment, Mrs. Van der Elst. As I go to school, these publicity cards stare out at me from house windows. Now that Thelma's hair is short, I am wearing mine in ringlets, but I wish that my nose was not so big. I had to go straight from school to have the photograph taken and the collar of my school blouse is not lying straight and there's even a fraction of gymslip in the picture. My only consolation is that I have not got a stye. Some time ago somebody told me to rinse my eyes twice a day with an eye bath filled with eye lotion. "Don't buy Optrex," she said. "Make up a lotion yourself of boracic crystals and water and keep it in a bottle. Do this for two years and you'll never have another stye."

50

Mrs. Williams is one of Mother's church cronies. She is older than my mother and very tall and thin with pretty blue eyes and rosy cheeks. She is the mother of Eric Williams who is the boy who won a scholarship the same year as I won mine. Coming home from school he is sometimes walking down Finch Lane at the same time as me after we get off the tram. He is stuffing his school cap into his pocket as I am squashing my school hat into my school bag. We both know that, as the only two pupils in school uniform in the whole of the housing scheme, without the hats we are less likely to draw attention to ourselves and be forced into pretending that we do not hear the shouts of "College Pudden". Mrs. Williams tells Mother that Eric has one of these photographs of me on the wall of his bedroom. I do not have the attention of any boyfriend and I have not the slightest idea of how to encourage such attention, but I am quite flattered by the fact that I have an admirer. I do wish that he was not just so tall and thin so that walking beside him I feel as if I am looking up at a lamp-post.

The Rose Queen event takes place and my hair is cut and permed especially for the occasion. There are many photographs and that night I am allowed to attend the special Rose Queen Social. I am told that throughout my year as Rose Queen I can attend the sixpenny socials and the twopenny film shows free of charge. To further mark the event I am presented with two white prayer books. The one my mother gives me is leather with gold lettering, and the one I receive from the church is backed in white ivory. Both of these prayer books have been printed just prior to the coronation and in the prayer for the Royal Family we are praying for our new King Edward VIII.

This is the coronation that is never to take place. As I begin my reign the Prince of Wales is renouncing his claim to the throne in favour of a life of exile with Mrs. Wallace Simpson.

In August 1939 we are enjoying a long, hot summer. All the talk is of Germany, of Hitler, of Neville Chamberlain and his umbrella and of "Peace in our Time". From the wireless and the newspapers we learn that arrangements are being made for the evacuation of school children from all major cities which, in the event of war, could be the targets of enemy air raids.

Knowsley, where we live, is outside the city boundary but we receive word that the pupils of St Edmund's College are to be evacuated.

"You don't have to go," Mother says, "We live in a safe area. Besides you wouldn't want to miss your birthday."

As a special treat this year I am to be allowed to go on holiday to Auntie Lucy's house in Derbyshire. For my birthday, Mother gives me two very pretty floral sets of underskirts and panties, one in pink and the other yellow. I also have the two new dresses which Mother bought me for the church social functions, a floral dress and a powder blue. They were marked "To be dry-cleaned only" but Mother said "Rubbish" and washed them and the crêpy material shrank so that now they barely fit me. Even so, they get packed along with the new undies and my nightie for my first trip away from home on my own.

Mother sees me off on the train at Liverpool and Auntie Lucy meets me at the station as I arrive. At her house I am introduced to her gentleman boarder, an old man of about thirty. He eats his meals with us, and while we wait for Auntie Lucy to bring the food to the table he asks me what I have found to read on Auntie Lucy's shelf of books. I tell him I am reading *Famous Crimes of the Century*.

Each day I go for walks with Auntie Lucy. She knows everyone in Old Glossop. When Granddad Lowe was alive he had a chemist's shop in Glossop but he died before I was born.

"This is Gerald's daughter," she says as she gives me a cuddle. "She's just fifteen. She was a Rose Queen this year in Liverpool." Her friends look suitably impressed, if not by me at least by the mention of Liverpool. Many of the people I meet have strong Derbyshire accents which I find difficult to understand. On market days we go down to the local market to buy pork pie and brawn from Mary Bentley's stall, just as we did when Thelma and I came to Old Glossop years ago before Frank was born. Mary Bentley begins each remark with "Ee . . ." and her young niece will ask me, "Are you going to wash you?" and although I know what she means, I keep saying "Pardon" so I can hear her repeating this oddity of speech.

There is one wonderful day while I am staying with Auntie Lucy. I join with other children in the hay-making at a local farm. We have a great time romping in the hay and riding back to the farmhouse on top of the cart piled with hay. Tea at the farmhouse is the best I have ever tasted; lots of newly baked bread and butter and home-made raspberry jam.

When I return home, Mother has had a letter in reply to the one she wrote refusing my evacuation. It says, "The school term will begin as usual on September 10th when St Edmund's pupils who are already billeted in Chester will share the facilities of Queen's School. The school at Prince's Park, Liverpool, will remain closed."

"Where will I go to school?" I ask. "It's the beginning of my two year school certificate course."

On Sunday, September 3rd, we are sitting round the wireless in 95 Southdean Road. Neville Chamberlain's voice comes right into our living room. He talks about the ultimatum given to Hitler as his troops marched into Poland and ends "No such message has been received. As a result this country is at war with Germany."

I cannot help but feel a thrill of excitement, knowing that I am going to be alive during a war such as the Great War which Mother and Granddad so often talk about. Mother's two brothers, Jack and Willie, had been lost at sea in that war and Daddy's brother, Claud, was killed the day before hostilities ended. I look at the faces of Mother and Granddad and contain my excitement in order to assume the appropriately sad face.

54

That week Mother takes me, complete with suitcase, gas mask, school uniform and schoolbag, to Chester.

The school authorities inform us that most of the billets so generously offered by the townspeople of Chester have already been filled, but we are taken to 51 Gladstone Avenue where the Lloyd family, who already have one evacuee, are willing to accept a second. The Lloyds give us afternoon tea and show us the big front bedroom which their daughter Grace has vacated so that Nesta, the other evacuee, and I may comfortably share it.

Before she leaves, Mother says, "You are very lucky, Joan. It's obvious to me that you are going to be living with a very kind family. Mrs. Lloyd is paid ten shillings a week from the government for your keep which means she is keeping you for practically nothing. She is an elderly lady in her sixties and at her time of life she shouldn't have to be bothering with children at all. Make sure you do your share of helping, washing the dishes, setting the table, doing her messages. I'll try to send you a weekly parcel so be certain that whatever I send gets shared with the family. There's no way I can keep coming to see you and you'll settle in better if I don't."

Grace, the nineteen year old daughter, comes home from the police office where she works. She has short straight hair and looks very smart in her police uniform. She is a year older than Thelma but much less grown up and she talks to me as if we were both the same age. I like her immediately.

For the next few days, Nesta gets regular visits from her mother plus parcels. She opens the parcels in our bedroom, gives me one of her chocolate marshmallow biscuits and eats the rest herself. She shares nothing with the Lloyds. She cries a lot and the following weekend her parents come to take her home.

The Lloyds are concerned that they failed to make her happy with them and expect me to be adversely affected by her departure. This does not happen. My own opinion is that she is younger than me, an only child, and in my mother's words, "used to getting her own way".

Grace says, "So that you won't feel lonely I'll move back in with you. For me it will be like having a sister." Pretty, rosy-cheeked, white-haired Mrs Lloyd tuts and smiles her shy smile and says she had better see about changing the sheets. Grace says not to worry, she'll see to that and I can help her. Mr. Lloyd, retired chief inspector in the police force, smokes his pipe, saying "Don't worry, this war will be over by Christmas."

At nine o'clock he pours himself his bowl of rice crispies and adds the milk so that the contents of the bowl rise exactly to the point when they threaten to spill over the edge.

"Going to need to use the car on Monday," he says. "I've to go to court."

"You could drop me in town on your way," says Mrs Lloyd.

"I could," is Mr Lloyd's answer, "but am I going to? I'm leaving here before eight o'clock. Do you want to go into town then?"

56

"Please don't speak to me as if I were a child, Pennant. Of course I don't want to go into town a whole hour before the shops open. It's a foolish man you are to think I would."

There follows a short heated interchange between them in Welsh then Mrs Lloyd resumes her smiling face. Mr Lloyd takes himself off to bed and we three females talk about men in general and fathers in particular.

"Ooh!" says Grace, "you do rub him up the wrong way, Mother. You should know by now that he likes to be buttered up."

"Is it like that in your house, Joan?" asks Mrs Lloyd.

I hesitate. "Well, sometimes perhaps, but, you see, my Dad is home so little that both my parents make a big fuss of one another."

"How long have they been married?"

"They got married during the last war, so it's more than twenty years."

"About the same as you and Dad, Mother," Grace comments.

"Yes, but we were in our forties when we got married. Your mother must have been much younger."

"She was nineteen."

"Ooh, imagine that! I'd best start concentrating on getting some nice man for myself. How do you fancy Hywell Ap Yarwyth for a son-in-law, Mother?"

"Indeed to goodness, it's not for me to say, Gracie. It has to be you that fancies him, though I must say he's got a good job. He might even make a good husband."

Grace laughs. "He might at that but could I face being called Mrs Ap Yarwyth? It's a bit of mouthful, isn't it?"

I am to hear more about Hywell when we lie in bed chatting before we go to sleep.

"Hywell's a bit rum, you know."

"What does that mean?"

"Well, hot. You know, passionate. The way he kisses. I have to watch my step so as not to get him too roused."

I look forward to Friday nights. Out of her wages Grace buys our Friday treat; chocolate marzipan walnuts, which we eat in bed. Sweet rationing is not yet enforced and when the war ends this particular confection never makes a reappearance.

Saturday nights, when Grace goes to a dance or a cinema with Hywell, I lie in bed and hear them talking at the front gate. This goes on for so long that I usually fall asleep before Grace comes to bed and I have to wait until next morning to hear about the Saturday night passion.

On Sunday mornings, Mr Lloyd prepares his lesson for the adult Sunday School class which he teaches. He sits with his big family Bible and several concordances to which he constantly refers. Mrs Lloyd busies herself in the kitchen preparing the Sunday midday dinner. Grace floats around, with no make up, in a cotton dressing gown for the best part of the morning. Depending on her mood, she either settles herself in the bathroom to give her face a "good do" or else takes on the chore of giving the big Welsh dresser a "good do". My help is enlisted whatever the choice.

During the bathroom session I act as listener.

"Why in Heaven's name could I not have been given skin like my mother's? What do I get? A complexion as sallow and pocked as my father's." Then, while concentrating on squeezing the next blackhead, "You don't know how lucky you are; you never get so much as a single pimple."

"I used to get styes and boils. I would now if I didn't use an eyebath every morning."

"I can't believe that. How did you manage to keep your thick, dark eyelashes. You do know that they are your most enhancing feature, don't you? Look at mine; mousy just like my hair. I eat too many cream cakes, that's my trouble. I'll start tomorrow on some healthy eating."

If the Welsh dresser takes precedence over the blackheads, I can more actively help in removing all the china that decorates its front, the items brought home by Mr. Lloyd in his sea-going days, when he served in the Royal Navy. Grace washes all the dinner service and uses great vigour to polish the dresser before replacing the china. The job lasts about two hours and Grace talks throughout.

"My father was a naval engineer. I wish I had his brain instead of his complexion. He is planning to put a new back boiler in our fireplace and he'll do it all himself. He reads it all up and thinks about it for weeks before he makes a start and then he'll do the job better than any tradesman."

I think about my own father, who will happily scrub floors, make sandwiches and can get rid of the washing up while we are still clearing the table, but cannot even wire up an electric plug. Mother tells the story of how, when she was whitewashing the ceiling in the Smith Street kitchen overnight, my father went to bed. When she at last climbed into bed, he rose and did the clearing up so that, after he had brought her breakfast in bed next morning, she came down to find everything spotless.

Grace continues to talk. "He's a very determined man, my father and very regular in all his habits. He gives a tenth of his income to the Welsh Methodist church and he is highly respected by the Chester police and I know that because I work with them, don't I? Since he retired, he has worked as a magistrate. He gets a special petrol ration to enable him to drive into courts in North Wales and he wouldn't dream of using that petrol for private driving, no matter how much my mother pleads with him to use the car to drive them to church on a wet Sunday evening."

Sunday dinner is served and it is only when we reach the rice pudding that my tears are dropping into it.

"You don't have to finish it," Mrs. Lloyd says. "I suppose it isn't the same as your mother makes at home."

"It is," I manage to say between sniffs. "It's exactly the same. The whole dinner is the same, just as it is at home so I can't help thinking about them all sitting round the table and me not being there."

"You'll miss your sister," Grace says sympathetically."

"It's not her I miss. She's much more grown up than you and we quarrel. I miss my little brother. He's not five yet and I miss not seeing him."

"Don't you worry," Mr. Lloyd says. "The war will be over by Christmas."

Sunday afternoon is when Grace meets her girl friends by the river Dee. She takes me with her and for a while we sit on the benches, listening to the band playing.

"This is Joan, our evacuee. She is just fifteen and would you believe it, she is a Rose Queen. Joan, this is Edna. We were at school together."

"So, now you've got two evacuees?"

"Well, yes, we did have Nesta but we couldn't come up to Nesta's expectations. She was only with us for two weeks so, you see, we've lost our Welsh evacuee and, so far, we've kept the English one."

"So you are going to be sharing a building with the Queen's School," Edna says. "That's the school we went to."

"Until two years ago," Grace adds. "We matriculated together. What a power of work that was!"

"How does the sharing work out?" Edna asks. I tell her how we go to school until midday one week and the following week we are there from one to five o'clock so that we are alternating with the Queen's pupils.

"With your own teachers?"

"That's right," says Grace, "and as well as teaching they'll be popping in from time to time to make sure we are coming up to scratch."

"Coming up to scratch?"

"Well, you know, things like meals on time and are we giving our evacuee enough to eat."

"Are you homesick?"

"Only now and then."

"Her father is serving in the Merchant Navy so there's just her mother and her sister and her little brother Frank at home."

"And my Granddad. He comes up every Wednesday and Sunday. We used to live with him."

"Would you believe it? Her grandfather is only the same age as my parents."

"I expect you'll get a letter from your mother tomorrow. Next time she sees you, she'll say you've got fatter on Mrs. Lloyd's cooking."

"Oh, I nearly forgot, Edna. You're invited to tea on Wednesday. Can you make it?"

"Thanks, I hope so. I may have to work late and I won't know till Wednesday. Give me a ring at lunchtime."

"Are we going to see that Gary Cooper film at the Odeon this week?"

"What about Friday? Would you like to come with us, Joan?"

Sunday teatime is followed by my accompanying the Lloyds to the Welsh Methodist church where the sermon is preached in Welsh. Back home again, Grace says, "It's pretty boring for Joan listening to all that Welsh. It's bad enough for me. Can't we let her stay at home with a magazine?"

"Well, I don't know about that. What do you think yourself, Joan?"

"I'd be okay in the house by myself."

Mr. Lloyd says, "We can leave her in charge of stoking up the fire and then it won't matter how long the sermon is, we won't be coming home to find the fire nearly out as we are tonight."

Mrs Lloyd tuts her disapproval. "It's for Joan to decide. Stoke the fire indeed, what would her mother say if she heard you?" Despite herself, a smile crosses her face. "You wouldn't be lonely or nervous?"

I laugh, "I'm fifteen."

"We'll see how you feel about it next Sunday. Gracie will let you look at that magazine she gets each week. What's it called, Gracie, bach?"

"It's called *Nineteen*, Mother."

"A bit old for Joan," Mrs. Lloyd giggles, "but perhaps that won't matter too much. And while I remember, Grace, you've been stealing my raisins from my baking cupboard. That's too bad of you. They're getting scarcer in the shops. Tut, tut, a big grown-up girl like you still stealing her mother's raisins. You make me very cross."

Suddenly she smiles a very mischievous smile and turns to me, "I'm only pretending to be cross, you know. I don't really mind Grace stealing the raisins. You can steal them too if you want to."

It is Wednesday and I am about to go to morning school. Mrs Lloyd gives me a list of the things I am to buy from the grocer and baker for Edna's tea.

"I forgot to remind Grace to ring Edna," she adds, "so when you finish school you can ring from the public phones outside the town hall to make sure Edna is coming before you buy all the extras."

I leave Gladstone Avenue and linger at the canal, as I always do, to watch the water being released through the locks. I climb the stone steps up to the city walls which take me to school. When school is over I am with my friend, Joan Powell. I explain to her that I'm going to use the phone and collect the shopping. She suggests that we do the shopping first as Bridge Street is on our way to the town hall.

I purchase the tinned apricots, boiled ham, bridge rolls, cakes and cream. It is only when I am struggling to get inside the phone box with the two paper carriers that I remember why it is I have to make the phone call. I get through to Edna and say urgently, "Edna, you can come to tea tonight, can't you?"

"Yes, I can. Is anything wrong?"

I briefly explain and she laughs.

Later, we are all tucking into our tea when Edna tells the Lloyds about the phone call. They think the story quite hilarious.

64

"You need not have worried, Joan," Mrs. Lloyd says. "With Grace's appetite the extra food would not have been wasted."

I smile along with them but I am thinking how my mother might have reacted had I made the same mistake at home. The Lloyds are certainly more comfortably off than are the Lowe family.

"I'm going to the pictures with Morven, tonight," Grace announces, "Do you want to come with us or have you got too much homework?"

"Yes, please. I've done all my homework."

"Ooh, you don't get nearly as much homework as we got when I was fifteen. Get a move on, then, get your coat."

Grace and I walk into town up Canal Street. Always she is nodding or having a word with the numerous acquaintances that we meet en route. She is at ease with all age groups. We meet Morven outside the cinema and Grace pays me in. When the show is over, the three of us go down to the Plane Tree café where we sit another hour chatting over ice-cream sundaes, sprinkled with chopped nuts and melting under chocolate sauce.

Memorable of my stay in Chester is our walking the walls which surround the city and paying heed to the architecture of the cathedral. There, a Bishop Tubbs takes a small group of us for confirmation classes. A lovely man, he encourages us to question much of the faith and some of his answers and the openness of his advice remain with me long after the subsequent confirmation service in Liverpool proves disappointing.

Grace has a birthday party while I am in Chester and the Lloyds extend their hospitality to include several soldiers from the local barracks. We have the party in the Lloyds' home with Mr. Lloyd opening his own home-made potato wine which the guests insist is as potent as any whisky.

Such are the early months of the war in 1939. We carry our gas masks. We practise going into air-raid shelters at school. There is even the wail of the occasional siren followed minutes later by the All Clear. There is a trickle of school pupils back to Liverpool. The Autumn term ends and we are allowed to go home for the Christmas holiday.

As I had promised myself at an earlier Christmas, I polish the furniture, hang the decorations, dress the Christmas tree and tack the holly and mistletoe above the doorways hoping that, now I am fifteen, somebody might visit us that I could fancy as much as I do the butcher boy who delivers Mrs. Lloyd's orders or the six foot five soldier they called Lofty, who was quite the most handsome guest at Grace's party.

With Christmas over I return to Chester but many pupils do not return and presently we learn that, with a skeleton staff, St Edmund's is re-opening in Liverpool. What had been a trickle becomes a flood and soon I am saying goodbye to the Lloyds who, for such a short while, have been my second family.

February 1940

My father is working in Glasgow and Mother decides that she is going to spend a few days with him. She leaves on the morning of February 13th, taking Frank with her. Armed with the housekeeping money, I purchase several Valentine cards, seal them with the letters S.W.A.L.K. (sealed with a loving kiss) written on the back of the envelopes and post them. Doubtlessly encouraged by the receipt of the Valentine cards, several of my friends approach me as I leave the Sunday morning church service.

"I hear your Mum is up in Glasgow. How about inviting us round to your house for the evening?"

I can hardly refuse. It is common practice that we take it in turns to tip one another off so that, as parents are out at a whist drive or fire-watching or Home Guard duty, we move into that home to play harmless games of Brag, Poker and Pontoon and indulge in a spot of table-tapping.

"Okay, you can come tomorrow night."

On Monday, Thelma and I lay in supplies of butter puffs, lemon curd and lemonade, all out of the housekeeping money. I open the door to a group of seven or eight people. As the evening progresses, the guests become a little boisterous and the leg of the table gives way. It is the old gate-legged table we brought from Smith Street.

"Don't worry," they say, "we'll come back and mend it before your mother comes home."

It is Wednesday and Granddad is coming for his mid-week visit. We prop the table up with books and cover the whole thing with a cloth which almost reaches the floor. In the middle of tea, there is a knock at the door. I open it to see a number of smiling faces.

"We're back to mend the table."

"You can't come in," I say.

"Oh, come on!"

"Go away."

"What about the table?"

"Well, right now my granddad's sitting, eating his tea off it."

"Okay, we'll be back."

They are, every night for the rest of the week. The table leg is glued into place while more butter puffs and lemonade disappear.

Mother comes home and is shocked by our budget account, doctored to disguise how the money had actually been spent. She doesn't notice that the table leg is held up with glue.

I am amazed. This ever-wise Mother of mine is fallible. I realise that, despite still living at home under her hitherto all-seeing eye, with one's peers it is possible to lead an independent life over which it would seem she has no control. It is this awareness that leads me to appreciate that childhood is nearing its end. I am becoming an adolescent.

For the rest of the war I am a very naïve adolescent, reared in an age when most of my contemporaries are as naïve as me. I go to see the Judy Garland and Deanna Durbin films and in my mind I identify with them. There is one big difference; they have an unlimited wardrobe while I am still growing and, with few clothing coupons up to the end of the war and beyond, am still wearing the pinafore skirt the twins made for my fourteenth birthday, my school blazer and navy blue gym knickers. At one point my father gives up his Merchant Navy clothing coupons so that my wardrobe may be supplemented to take me to training college. We have to spend them in the men's department so both my trench coat and my striped pyjamas button across from left to right. We have no talcum powder and no nylons. In summer we paint our legs to look as if we are wearing stockings. The paint comes off on the white cotton sheets.

In May 1940 we are all believing in the miracle of Dunkirk.

At school, the topic that we most discuss is not the war but the Wednesday night radio programme. We sing the signature tunes from Bandwagon and, later, from Tommy Handley's ITMA (It's that man again!). We mimic all the catch phrases: "Ta-ta for now" and "Can I do you now, sir?"

Outside school, too, there are interests other than the war. I am not yet sixteen and I have a boy-friend. His name is Tony Almond and he works as a junior clerk in the fruit market. Mother refers to him as "the nut" and Granddad has christened him "the onion merchant". I met him at one of the church socials because, since I returned from being evacuated to Chester, I have resumed my Rose Queen status from last June so I don't have to pay the sixpence entry fee to the Tuesday church social. All the girls are enamoured with Tony and he spreads his affections widely.

He wears a trilby and, when he calls for me and when I open the door, he stands on the step, doffing his hat for all the world like Cary Grant or Mickey Rooney.

"See you when we see you," he confidently calls out to my family as we depart for the cinema.

"See you at ten-thirty and not a minute later, young man," comes my father's voice from the kitchen.

"Yes, sir. Of course, sir," is the smart response.

It lasts only weeks but I have a Valentine card and a toffee paper to keep his memory green while I wait and hope for him to renew the romance.

"Oh, oh, Antonio, he's gone away.
He's left me on my ownio, all on my ownio."

This and "Our love affair has been such fun" are the songs my father sings as he passes me in the depths of my heartbreak.

It is a Sunday morning when I discover that I have been replaced in Tony's affections by Olive Wilson, a dowdy little dwarf in my opinion.

Waiting for Sunday dinner, barely able to hold back the tears, I am seeking refuge behind a magazine. My father, looking up from his Sunday paper, demands to know whose these shoes are, lying, waiting to be put away. No-one answers him so he repeats the question in a more irritable tone. Thelma comes to my defence. "They're Joan's shoes but she's upset. Best leave her

70

alone." My father wants to know since when has she been the best judge of that. She answers back, the unforgivable sin, and so becomes the target for his ill humour. A battle ensues during which I roughly seize the offending shoes. One of the shoes slips from my grasp and hurls itself in the direction of my father. It strikes his open newspaper which rips down the full length of the page. The tears that I held back come flooding out and, amid the chaos, there is a knock at the door.

My mother shouts from the kitchen, "Thelma, Joan, will someone open the door?"

I get to the door to see the faces of Jack and Emily Jobson, who usually appear as part of a threesome, with their elderly mother, about one Sunday each year.

I'm dabbing frantically at the tears, trying to smile a greeting as I usher them in.

"Oh, hello, Emmy, Jack, what a lovely surprise. How's Auntie Sadie?"

They are shocked into silence for a moment, then, in hushed tones, "She's dead, Joan. She died a year ago. We wrote to tell you."

Of course. I remember. The embarrassment of this moment on top of everything else overcomes me. I rush upstairs and throw myself into the bathroom, where I stay until I am called down for dinner.

It is a tragi-comic moment which, over the years, crystallizes into a gem of black humour. In the middle of the high-ding-dong of some family argument, one of us will slip unnoticed to the front door, open and close it to create a lull while saying, loudly and clearly, "Oh, hello, Emmy, Jack, how nice to see you." As the din within subsides into silence, then is the time to re-enter alone, with a secret smile, provoking everyone to collapse with relief and accompanying laughter. It never fails.

By the late summer of 1940, war is on the doorstep with the Battle of Britain. Most food items are rationed and we are restricted to a minimum number of clothing coupons.

Thelma buys two-ply wool, of which four ounces will knit a lacy, short-sleeved jumper. She is saving her coupons to buy a winter coat. It is a beautiful new coat but she accidentally gets a hedge tear on the cuff and it has to go into the dry cleaners so that it can be invisibly repaired. The cleaners is wiped out in an air-raid and she loses the coat. In wartime there is no form of compensation for either cost or coupons.

We sample Spam as a replacement for cold meats, which are rationed, and we regularly breakfast off dried egg. Frequently the siren sounds as we are sitting down to eat our evening meal. Mother takes Frank out with her to the Anderson shelter but Thelma says she is not going without her tea. When the sirens sound later in the evening, Mother and Frank sleep in the shelter while Thelma and I go to our beds. Mother attempts to remonstrate with us but, as time goes on and the nights get colder, Mother puts Frank into his bright blue siren suit and they take shelter in a cupboard under the stairs.

Granddad, like many other people, says, "If the bomb has got your name on it, you'll be hit wherever you are so you might as well die in your comfortable bed." If it is a bad raid he sometimes has to stay overnight, as do other friends who may be visiting. Air-raid wardens patrol the streets and transport comes to a halt. During the first weeks of the raids, cinemas and theatres have to be vacated until the All Clear sounds but as the raids become heavier and more frequent such places are closed down.

Every day the newspaper headlines tell us the number of enemy planes that have been brought down on the previous day. We know that our pilots are successful in the night raids because they eat carrots which help them see better in the dark.

At the height of the Blitz, Everton Valley is reduced to ashes. This happens on a Saturday night. There is no public transport so on the Sunday morning Thelma cycles down to find, amid the smoke and rubble and the acrid smell from the burnt-out jam factory, the police are barring her way into Smith Street. She insists and reaches my grandfather. He is standing in the middle of a roofless, windowless 86 Smith Street, dazed and bewildered, clutching the two slices of bacon which he has salvaged from the wreckage. He comes to live with us. He loses his home and his business and there is no form of compensation. Because he has been self-employed he does not qualify for a state pension.

Throughout the day, public transport is disorganised, re-routed without notice to avoid fire and flood damage, and eventually I am allowed a permanent late pass which excuses me from school assembly. Miss Wilson, the deputy head who regularly presides over assembly, confronts me one day concerning my late arrival. I explain about the two buses which I have to take to school and show her my late pass. She is disgusted. "Anyone who cannot get to school on time despite adverse conditions does not deserve the honour of being a prefect."

The same lady is a splendid history teacher. She can talk for half an hour on a topic and only two headings will be written on the blackboard. She teaches us to sub-divide under such main headings so that the brief notes we take are easily memorised. I am one of the many in my year who are indebted to her for the School Certificate distinctions in History which we later manage to achieve.

She also teaches religious knowledge. We are required to study the Book of Amos and find equivalent examples of corruption in present day society. Barbara, one of my class mates, has neglected to do the set homework. When, without warning, she has to cite a current malaise, she invents a story of oranges being dumped at the docks. She continues to fabricate answers to the cross-questioning that ensues so finally Miss Wilson is preparing her letter of complaint to the official authorities and Barbara is hoping that her father who works at the docks does not lose his job.

Miss Wilson, by a few vivid strokes, conjures up for us a picture of John the Baptist in the wilderness, living on locusts. In later life when I encounter the story again it is not John the Baptist I see but Miss Wilson, a

74

striking figure herself, tall and erect with iron-grey hair and wearing her green overall over her gown, forever fingering the chalk which she so seldom used.

As part of our School Certificate course, all pupils sit a diocese examination which, together with questions on Old and New Testaments, will contain a section on Church of England doctrine. The school chaplain who teaches this, unlike Bishop Tubbs in Chester, is so dull and boring that behind propped up school bags most of his class are taking the opportunity to catch up with homework.

I willingly take part in English lessons which are taught by Miss Potter. She has an Eton crop and dresses in a masculine way in heavy brogues and tailored suits which appear in mustard, wine and powder blue. She opens up a world of literature to us. She encourages us to act out the characters from *As You Like It* and *Julius Caesar* and, herself, brings the principal figures to life. She shares with us the delights of poetry and prose and is responsible for my second distinction in School Certificate.

I work very hard in this my fifth year at secondary school. In the final examination it is necessary to qualify in all nine subjects so, in addition to those already mentioned, we study English Language, Geography, Botany, Zoology, Maths, French and Art.

Most of the girls in my class are leaving at the end of this year. I decide that I, too, will leave.

My mother says, "I thought you were going to stay on a sixth year and qualify to go to teacher-training college."

"I've changed my mind. All my friends are leaving."

"That's up to you, of course. You'll need to explain your change of mind to your teachers."

So I attempt to do this.

"What are you planning to do when you leave school?"

"I want to work in a journalist's office with a view to becoming a writer."

"You'll only have a year before you are eligible to be called up for national service. You won't be doing anything except making the tea. Stay on at school for another year and at eighteen you can get accepted for teacher training. Two years at college and you'll be a qualified teacher and in your spare time you can write all you want."

It sounds wonderful. I do not foresee that the "spare time" will prove to be a myth.

As the school breaks up for the summer holidays Miss Wilson announces that she is looking for volunteers from senior girls to form a fruit-picking party to help the war effort. I decide this is one way to earn a little money.

We make our own way to the Smedleys' farm near Worcester. At the station there is much teasing and somebody dares me to buy the child's half price train ticket.

"You haven't even got the beginnings of a figure. You could easily pass for fourteen."

I think of my father who regularly slips a tasty tit-bit to the policeman at the docks as he is passing through with some of the ship's left-overs to supplement our meagre rations. He will laugh when I tell him about the ticket and say I'm a chip off the old block. I succumb to the dare.

About twenty girls assemble at the house where we are to board. There is a kitchen, a dining room with the bare necessities of table and chairs and three or four bedrooms where we are to sleep on mattresses on the floor.

In high spirits we are anticipating the evening meal. It consists of one course; a spinach omelette. Most of us are unable to finish it and are consequently upbraided for the sin of wasting food which our brave sailors have risked life and limb to bring to our ports.

"I used twelve eggs for your meal," Miss Wilson states. I think how much more I would have enjoyed half a boiled egg.

We rise early the next morning. For breakfast we are given tea and two slices of bread. We walk for an hour to reach the fruit orchards and we find it an intolerable time to lunch. We sample the loganberries which we have been assigned to pick, but they are not very filling. When the lunches are unpacked we each receive one round of Marmite sandwiches. I hate the smell of Marmite but force myself to eat them.

At four o' clock our baskets of fruit are weighed and we receive our measly cash reward. We trail the hour's walk back to the house, tired and hungry. There are five loaves on the table. They are consumed within minutes and we must wait until seven o'clock for the evening meal. The single course is a vegetable stew, chiefly beans. There are neither potatoes nor bread to fill our empty stomachs. Once again the meal is scarcely edible because it has been burnt. Much of it is left uneaten.

As on the previous evening Miss Wilson selects her two helpers for the following day who will accompany her to Worcester to carry the shopping and help prepare the evening meal. She expresses her disgust at the greed of twenty girls who between them ate five large loaves at tea-time and were therefore unable to eat the meal she had spent time cooking. In future at tea-time we will be rationed to one slice each.

Upstairs we seek out the helpers chosen for the morrow and give them money to buy buns for us when they are in Worcester. At least we will not be hungry tomorrow night.

The next morning we come down to burnt porridge. There is much left over so for the rest of the week we alternate between cold stew and cold porridge sandwiches. Daily we supplement our diet with buns.

Two weeks go by and the last Saturday arrives. After the final evening meal, it is reckoning time. Miss Wilson sits behind a cash box at the head of the table. She informs us that from our meagre earnings she expects each of us to pay over a percentage to cover the fares and additional expenses of herself and her two daily helpers who by shopping and cooking had thus forfeited their fruit-picking wages. In addition she demands a sum of money for our food and accommodation.

We are dismayed. Most of us will be left with nothing after a fortnight of hard slog and near starvation. We have no choice but to pay over the money and wait while it is counted and recounted several times. Miss Wilson then announces that she is one pound short. There is a thief in our midst. No-one is allowed to leave the dining room until the pound is replaced or the thief confesses.

Hours later we are still sitting at the dining table. Miss Wilson then decides that she will retire to another room and we in turn will go to her in private and account for every penny we possess. This ordeal goes on long after dark. Her organised search of the bedrooms reveals the buns which we had ordered so we face a very angry woman as we singly account for the cash in our purses.

When my turn comes, I am forced to explain that my extra cash comes as a result of travelling half fare on the railway. I have my return ticket to prove it.

"You are a liar and a thief," she storms. "I will be writing to your parents to inform them of your disgraceful behaviour."

I say, "You don't have to do that. I'll tell them myself."

"In view of what you have done, it is hardly likely that I am going to trust you to keep your word."

No-one is allowed to leave the house on the Sunday and the pound is never found. The two Catholic girls in the party are in tears because they are not allowed to attend Sunday Mass and that is a sin.

We return home. I tell my mother about the whole nightmare experience. The following day an open postcard arrives from Miss Wilson. "This is to inform you that your daughter travelled half fare on the railway thereby proving herself to be a liar and a thief."

My mother explodes, not at me for my misconduct which I have already confessed, but at the indignity of receiving an open postcard, with no preliminary form of address, which anyone including the postman could have read.

I don't know to whom my mother addresses her letter of reply; it may be Miss Wilson or it may be the headmistress. I do know that in it she said that her daughter had lost a stone in weight during the fortnight and that the teacher in charge was no fit person to be responsible for the welfare of young girls.

Within a day or two of coming back to Liverpool, I receive my school certificate results. On the strength of my distinction in History I plan to make it one of my sixth year subjects. How can I do this if Mother sends the letter? I may no longer be a child; my mother may be superfluous to the decisions I think I am capable of making for myself, but no amount of pleading on my part can persuade her to refrain from posting it.

I wish I could say that as life went on I was later to prevail in battles with my mother. I wish I could say that I grew stronger in character and she grew weaker. I was never a match for my mother. With her complete mental faculties, she lived to within ten days of being ninety years old and, although she will never read it, over many years I have written these memories of my Liverpool childhood as a tribute to her.

AFTERWORD

What became of Miss Wilson? Letter or no letter, she was sufficiently professional and lacking in rancour to tutor Joan Lowe when she was the only sixth year pupil continuing to study history.

After two more years of the war spent at teacher-training college, Joan taught for eight years in Liverpool until she married Alexander Park and moved to Glasgow. There she continued to teach thus becoming one of the comparatively few working mothers of the early 1960s.

In retirement with five grandchildren, ages ranging from under one year to twenty three, it is only recently she has found the leisure to write about the childhood memories she shares with Thelma and Frank and her friend Eric who still live on Merseyside.

**The first part of Joan Park's memoirs
is also available in the
ISIS Large Print Reminiscence Series:**

86 SMITH STREET

Joan Park

*A memoir that recaptures ordinary family life in 1930s
Britain*

Daughter of a ship steward and a housewife, Joan Park
gives a delightful glimpse of her childhood from 1927
to 1941, when she and her family lived at 86 Smith
Street in Liverpool.

From the descriptions of her granddad's shoe repair
shop to the stories her mother used to tell, Joan Park
recounts her personal memories of the time of the
Great Depression with a child's innocent eye. This is
life as she encountered it in those days — family,
friends, school and the little incidents — all of which
had a big part to play in the day-to-day life of a little
girl growing up in Liverpool.

ISBN 0-7531-9842-8 (hb)
ISBN 0-7531-9843-6 (pb)

ISIS publish a wide range of books in large print, from fiction to biography. Any suggestions for books you would like to see in large print or audio are always welcome. Please send to the Editorial department at:

ISIS Publishing Ltd.
7 Centremead
Osney Mead
Oxford OX2 0ES
(01865) 250 333

A full list of titles is available free of charge from:
Ulverscroft large print books

(UK)
The Green
Bradgate Road, Anstey
Leicester LE7 7FU
Tel: (0116) 236 4325

(Australia)
P.O Box 953
Crows Nest
NSW 1585
Tel: (02) 9436 2622

(USA)
1881 Ridge Road
P.O Box 1230, West Seneca,
N.Y. 14224-1230
Tel: (716) 674 4270

(Canada)
P.O Box 80038
Burlington
Ontario L7L 6B1
Tel: (905) 637 8734

(New Zealand)
P.O Box 456
Feilding
Tel: (06) 323 6828

Details of **ISIS** complete and unabridged audio books are also available from these offices. Alternatively, contact your local library for details of their collection of **ISIS** large print and unabridged audio books.